RVing North to Alaska

Guide for RV Travel on the Alcan Highway

3rd Edition
Updated for the 2017 Travel Season

Rich and Gloria Eskew

Shoppe Foreman Publishing
Guthrie, Oklahoma

Copyright © 2014 by A. Richard Eskew and Gloria J. Eskew. All U. S. and international rights reserved. No part of this book may be reproduced or stored in any form or by any means without the prior written consent of the author, excepting brief passages used in reviews.

Cover and interior photos provided by the authors.

Published by
Shoppe Foreman Publishing
Guthrie, Oklahoma, U.S.A
www.ShoppeForeman.com

Printing/manufacturing information for this book may be found on the last page.

ISBN-13: 978-1542507646
ISBN-10: 1542507642

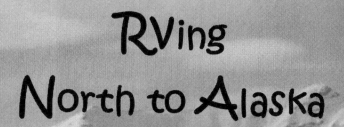

RVing North to Alaska

Guide for RV Travel on the Alcan Highway

3rd Edition
Updated for the 2017 Travel Season

Rich and Gloria Eskew

Contents

Acknowledgements 1
Preface 2
Introduction and Assumptions 3
Technical Considerations 6
    Planning the Trip 6
    Reservations 11
    Before You Leave 11
    Getting There 14
    Border Crossing 19
    Traveling in Canada 23
    The Alcan Highway 33
    Mechanical & Operational Considerations ... 35
    Other Tips and Suggestions 55
    Mileage and Facilities 63

Highlights along the Way 67
- Edmonton to Dawson Creek 70
- Dawson Creek to Fort Nelson 75
- Fort Nelson to Watson Lake 82
- Watson Lake to Whitehorse 90
- Whitehorse to Beaver Creek 94
- Alaska Border to Fairbanks 100

Updates for 2017 Travel Season 104
Appendix I: Publications and Websites 109
Appendix II: List of RV Parks 112
Index 115
About the Authors 117

Rich and Gloria Eskew

Acknowledgements

We want to say thank you to Ken and Gerry Gray, Springfield, Missouri, for their suggestions and especially for their encouragement. We cannot forget to mention the efforts of Chuck Gray, Fairbanks, Alaska.

Rich and Gloria Eskew

Preface

"You come to get rich, that's a damn good reason..." so penned by Robert Service in his masterpiece *The Spell of the Yukon*. Today, the visitor to Alaska may not reap the wealth of gold nuggets, but there are countless treasures just waiting to be claimed.

A trip to Alaska can change your life forever. You will meet a different stock of gutsy, rustic individuals prepared to assist you in every way necessary, stir your imagination with tales of how they came to be Alaskan, and offer the shake of friendship which will forever transcend any distance.

Be prepared to be enthralled by magnificent vistas from the meandering creeks, the mighty rivers, rolling hills running to the horizons, and soaring peaks of snow-capped mountains. Take it all in and capture the grandeur in your soul to be there for countless hours of memories. Once in Alaska, this Great Land becomes a part of you forever.

Introduction and Assumptions

This book is provided to give all who wish to travel to Alaska some basic guidelines to make their travel safe, memorable, and truly the trip of a lifetime. We have arranged these pages into two sections:

Technical Considerations

Highlights along the Way

We do not seek to advise you on what to see or what to do. There are countless brochures to give you a full lifetime of choices that you may wish to experience. We seek to give you as much information as possible for the preparation and the planning of your trip as well as to provide guidelines to avoid those nasty obstacles which could hinder your enjoyment.

In this book we seek to gather all of our experiences since our first Alcan trip way back in 1964. As of this writing, we have driven the Alcan forty-one one-way trips or, put another way, collectively we have traveled the Alcan seventy-three times. Our trips have been made in sedans, and we have slept in the backs of pickups and cargo trailers. Today, we consider our RV travel trailer a real luxury.

If you are an experienced RV traveler, please overlook any of the ultra-basic points that we make. It is not our intention to place you in a category of those who know nothing or those who know it all.

Because you are reading this, we assume that you will be traveling by means of a recreation vehicle of some sort to Alaska. While we are concentrating on your trip of a lifetime over the Alcan Highway to the last Great Frontier, most everything in this book will apply to any RV experience.

Be aware that we do not have personal, hands-on experience with RVs other than the travel trailer. As such, we may be leaving out items and issues which pertain specifically to Class A, Class C, fifth wheels. and other recreational vehicles. It would be foolish on our part to try to advise anyone with respect to recreational travel by any means other than a travel trailer.

We make the assumption(s) that you, the reader, are not familiar with such things as wheel bearings, brake controllers, shackles, and other mechanical specifics of your RV. Also, we assume you would like to have route guidelines for travel in the U.S., where to cross the border into Canada, along with any and all recommendations to make your trip the best possible.

You may seek arrangements to travel in a caravan and for some this is an excellent way to make the trip to Alaska. For us, the adventuring type, we take joy in the freedom of traveling alone – to come and go as we please; waiting on no one and no one is waiting on us. While we are not positive of the actual cost of traveling via a caravan, we are willing to put our best foot forward and say that we can do it for considerably less and enjoy the freedom of traveling without encumbrances.

Technical Considerations

Planning the Trip

One of the first considerations you must approach is the time of year for your trip to Alaska. You have a full 12 months of the year to choose from as the Alcan Highway is open year-round. However, the difficulties inherent with winter travel preclude almost everyone from enjoying the travel experience during the cold, harsh winter days.

From our experience, the best travel months are May through August. We try to avoid the Canadian Rockies prior to 15 May because of the possibility of a late winter/early spring snowfall. We consider snow to be a four-letter word. On our way back out to the Lower Forty-Eight we try to be on the east side of the mountains before 15 August.

Also in play with respect to the time of year, will be the duration of your trip. Consider the distance from Kansas City to Fairbanks is just short of 4,000 miles. If you drive 500 miles each day your one-way trip will take eight days. Then, consider the return trip and you are sixteen days on the road. While that may seem like an excessive amount of driving time, remember this is your once in a lifetime trip. The sights and scenery along the way are well worth the drive time.

Another consideration, which you may not have thought of, is taking advantage of the weather conditions you may or may not encounter along the way. For example, if the weather cooperates and it is beautiful with gorgeous sunshine and warm days on your way to Alaska, you may wish to spend more time stopping at various locations along the way. The reason we mention this is there is no guarantee you will have the same weather conditions on your return trip.

We assume that you already have an RV along with adequate experience in your home away from home. However, if you are planning to purchase your first RV, there are many things you should consider. Of prime importance is the type of RV and possibly what tow vehicle will be required.

Some may say that it would be best to purchase an RV and take several trips before venturing to the land of the midnight sun. This is probably very good advice. At the same time, with proper preparation and a good dose of common sense, there is no reason to forgo your trip just because you have no prior experience. We did it. We set out for Alaska pulling our first RV, a travel trailer, with no prior RV experience. Minor problems were encountered, primarily due to our lack of experience, but the trip was a great success.

If you have no prior experience with the world of RV travel, you will need to do a bit of homework prior to purchasing your vehicle as well as obtaining knowledge to make your trip pleasant and memorable. You'll need to pick the brains of those at your RV dealership, including the maintenance and service personnel. There is another source of information readily available to you at any time. No matter where you live, there is probably an RV park fairly close by. Take a drive to any RV park, most any time, introduce yourself to the folks staying there and explain your desire for information about the RV experience. For sure, you will find everyone more than willing to assist you and speak for hours about their personal experiences. While this method may seem to be a bit off-the-cuff, you will receive honest, forthright answers to your questions.

If you are relatively new to the wonderful world of the RV experience, you may wish to secure an excellent book on the basics: *RVing Basics*, by Bill and Jan Moeller, Ragged Mountain Press, Camden, Maine (available on Amazon).

Place yourself at the RV dealership with a bright sun reflecting off all the new vehicles awaiting your inspection and final selection. The salesman approaches with a smile as big as a mile, greeting you with a glad shake and a promise for great days ahead. One of his or her first questions should be: "What type of vehicle do you have to be your tow vehicle?" If this question is not presented right away put your guard up as this is an indication you're dealing with someone who just wants to sell.

Let's assume you will be selecting a thirty-foot

travel trailer with two slides. You plan to pull this rig with a half ton, gas-powered pickup. Now, there are advertisements that lead one to believe that this is totally acceptable. We don't believe them, and neither should you. The amount of weight by any travel trailer, or fifth wheel is significantly out of bounds for a half-ton pickup. We know: We did it! We will not do it again! Note: we are speaking with respect to full-size RV trailers and not small trailers such a Coleman pop-up.

On your trip to and from Alaska you will rack up more than 8,000 miles. You do not need to encounter a breakdown due to an overheated transmission, a worn rear wheel bearing, etc. Start off on the right foot and use a minimum three-quarter ton diesel pickup. Travel is relatively easy throughout much of the Lower Forty-Eight. However, there are many multi-mile slopes to climb in states such as Wyoming and Montana. And then, there are some significant hills to climb in the Canadian Rockies. We tend to call these "slow me downs." You need adequate power and performance which will not fail.

Reservations

Do you need to make reservations at the RV parks on the Alcan? We have been traveling the Alcan since '64 and never made a reservation. Over the past few years RV travel on the Alcan has diminished in sheer numbers. So you should have no difficulties on the Alcan. However, RV travel in the Lower Forty-Eight may be a moose of a different color. If you know how far you will travel on any given day, and you know where you want to stop for the night, then by all means make the reservation. There should be no cost to do so, and you will eliminate the anxiety of finding a pillow place for the night.

Before You Leave

How many times have you heard (or said yourself): "I wish someone had told me," or "I wish I had known that ahead of time?" Well, in the following pages we will try to provide some answers to questions you may not have thought about.

RV Manuals. If you are purchasing a new RV, be sure to have all relevant manuals with you. Do not rely on a promise from the salesperson that selected manuals, information, and other pertinent information will be forthcoming.

Medications. If you are taking prescriptions on a regular basis, it would be best to make sure you have an adequate supply before you leave. If necessary, make arrangements with your physician and/or pharmacy to carry extra meds with you or make arrangements for meds to be mailed or shipped. Also, take detailed information regarding all medications you take. No matter the circumstances, having such information on hand may eliminate several phone hours seeking to know exactly how many milligrams have been prescribed.

Secure a copy of your prescription for eye glasses. Lost or damaged eyewear can be easily and economically replaced if an examination is not required.

Road Hazard Service/Insurance. We have kept our enrollment with the Good Sam Club for several years. The Good Sam RV Parks provide quality facilities that meet or exceed our needs. Also, we like the discounts. In all of our travels we have called on Good Sam Road Service one time. Our experience was fantastic, and they lived up to their promises without any hassles. We highly recommend you explore joining this RV support entity.

When seeking to contract for a roadside assistance service it is very important to make sure the service provider will tow both vehicles if necessary. In the event your tow vehicle is out of service and needs towing, what happens to your RV trailer? Be sure your emergency road service provider will have the capabilities to tow both vehicles. Further, their operations must include service in Canada and Alaska. To be sure, get it in writing – don't assume and don't take the word of someone on the phone.

Photocopies. We may be a bit on the ultra-fastidious side of things when it comes to trying to cover all the bases, but we believe there can never be too much attention paid to the "worst case scenario." Accordingly, we photocopy a lot more paperwork than most folks. Here is a partial list of paperwork we photocopy:

- Passports
- Driver's license
- Vehicle registrations
- All insurance papers
- Small animal certificate
- Each credit card
- Prescriptions (medicine and vision)

In addition to the above, we keep a list of addresses and telephone numbers for those friends and relatives to whom we might want to send a post card or talk with on the phone. Whether we travel or not, it is a good idea to periodically make a list of contacts and the information in our cell phones. Once or twice a year we do the same with those on our e-mail contact list. While it is not probable, it is possible that a cell phone may get lost in the water or fly off to that land of mystery where every lost item waits for rescue.

Getting There

The first night of our annual trip to Alaska finds us camped out at an RV park in Boonville, Missouri.

RVing North to Alaska

We stop there every year to visit with relatives and the short run allows us to depart at a leisurely, no-rush time frame. So, this seems like a good spot to identify how we and others might travel to reach the beginning of the Alcan Highway at Dawson Creek, British Columbia.

All of you will come from different originating towns and cities across the country. For want of another way to encompass every route on every highway, let's start by using Kansas City as a somewhat geographical center of the Lower Forty-Eight.

From Boonville, Missouri, we travel west on I-70 heading to Kansas City. We continue on interstates around Kansas City by taking I-435 North, which leads us to I-29 heading to St. Joseph. We stay on Interstate I-29 following the western border of Iowa past Omaha and spend the night at the little town of Sloan, Iowa. We found there is a casino just to the west of the town of Sloan which allows RV parking for about $10 a night (note: electricity only). It is a nice break for us as we get our travel legs in good working order. If you do stop at this location, be sure to check out the lower cost of fuel due to the Native American tax considerations.

Our second day of travel finds us continuing on I-29 to Sioux Falls, South Dakota where we turn west on I-90. We have found over the years that I-90 is a good road with more than sufficient RV stopping points along the way. In comparison, when traveling across Nebraska on I-80 we have found fewer places to stop and a large portion of the road is a nightmare for us as it feels like a washboard.

You might want to take note of some of the attractions you pass along the way, such as the Corn Palace in Mitchell, South Dakota, or Badlands National Park, Mount Rushmore National Park, and Deadwood – places to become destinations for future trips.

Now that we are ancient geezers, we no longer rack up days with 800 miles or more rolling under our feet. Now-a-days, 500 miles is about all we want for a day. Our next night's stay will probably find us at the small town of Presho, South Dakota, relaxing at the New Frontier Campground. This RV park is one of the many affiliated with the Good Sam Club and fits our needs with respect to our daily distance goals. We try to stay at the same places each year as it reduces the anxiety of "where do we stay tonight" as part of the RV experience.

Continuing west from Sioux Falls, we stay on I-90 all the way to the west side of South Dakota. As a caution, if you are traveling around the first week of August you may wish to avoid the Sturgis Rally week with its many thousands of motorcycles. Also, during Rally week, all available camping facilities in the area will cost an arm and a leg.

We turn north at Spearfish and go north to Belle Fourche and then northwest on Highway 212 and spend the night at Broadus, Montana. (The RV park office is located at the corner of the main cross roads, not at the RV campsite.) This little town has a very quiet, non-fancy RV park but it fits our needs with respect to how far we drive each day. From Broadus we continue on Highway 212 heading for I-90 where we pass Custer's Last Stand.

We continue on I-90 to Billings and then proceed on Highway 87 north to Roundup then to Grass Range where the highway turns west to Lewiston and eventually to Great Falls. From Great Falls we continue north on I-15 to Shelby where we turn west on Highway 2 to Cut Bank. We always fill up on fuel at this last stop in the U.S. and there is a nice RV park on the west side of the city. From Cut Bank we go north on Highway 213 and cross the border into Canada just south of Del Bonita, Alberta. From there, we go west heading towards Cardston where we connect with Highway 2 heading north to Fort Macleod. We continue on Highway 2 north all the way to Leduc just south of Edmonton. To avoid Edmonton, we take Highway 39 west at Leduc to the city of Devon. Beyond Devon, we continue north until we intersect with Highway 16 (avoid Highway 16 A, unless you want to drive through several towns and encounter lots of red and green lights.) We take Highway 16 west until we come to Highway 43 which we take north heading for Whitecourt. Depending upon how we feel, we generally stay at a Sagitawah RV park just on the west side of Whitecourt. However, this RV park may be full due to transient workers. If this RV park is full you might seek a night's stay at the Lion's RV Park on the east side of Whitecourt before continuing north.

The next day we continue on Highway 43 to Valley View, where Sherk's is an excellent RV park at Valley View. We then proceed to Grand Prairie and on to Dawson Creek – the start of the Alcan Highway.

We suggest you contact Travel Alberta Canada at www.travelalberta.com or call 1-800-ALBERTA and request their publication *Camping in Alberta*. This publication is geared specifically for tourists seeking to enjoy the RV/camping experience. In addition to identifying private RV parks, this publication also identifies provincial parks.

Border crossing

We have found over the years that a friendly but mature demeanor at the border crossing results in minimal delays. Most of the individuals who relate horror stories of lengthy delays, intense searches of vehicles, etc, have the personality of angry rhinos.

In the preceding chapter, "Getting There," our route takes you to a very small, out-of-the-way border crossing. For many years we traveled north from Great Falls to Shelby, Montana, and continued north on I-15 to Sweet Grass and crossed into Canada at Couts. For many years we sailed through the Canadian customs with minimal delays. However, after the tragedy of the Twin Towers the increased security measures brought about delays which were at times lengthy and very frustrating. Taking advice from some friends, we tried the route from Cut Bank to Del Bonita. We have yet to encounter any delays and we have actually enjoyed the brief stop and small talk chatting with the customs officials.

To be sure you have no delays and to minimize frustrations, we suggest that you inquire ahead of time as to the hours of operation at whichever border crossing you select. The crossing at Sweet Grass is open twenty-four hours a day. However, the crossing located at Del Bonita as well as many others are only open during the summer months from 8 a.m. to 8 p.m. Don't take our word for this, double-check the hours of operations online at

    http://en.wikipedia.org/wiki/List_of_Canada-United_States_border_crossings

To cross the border you will need a valid passport and proof of insurance for your tow vehicle and possibly for your RV. Also, it would be a very good idea to make sure you have the proper registration for both of your vehicles. Also, before you depart, stop at your insurance agent and secure a written rider to your insurance policy that will provide coverage while you are in Canada. Make sure the rider covers the total length of time for your trip.

If you are traveling with pets you will be required to show a current, up-to-date small animal certificate. The main concern of the customs and immigration officials is a valid shot for distemper and rabies. Also, you might want to have your dog vaccinated with the Bordetella vaccine which is administered to dogs to prevent kennel cough and is recommended if your dog will be socializing with other dogs. Most, if not all, kennels will require this vaccination.

If you are traveling with children who are not your biological offspring, such as grandchildren, nieces or nephews, be aware that each child must have their own individual passport. Do not have children included on an adult passport as it will make separate travel very complicated and maybe impossible. Also, you may be required to show documentation whereby you have authority and permission for the children to be with you.

Another important point concerns anyone who

has ever been convicted of driving under the influence (DUI). The Canadian government considers such a conviction as a felony and may deny your entry to their country. If you have a DUI conviction, we strongly suggest that you contact the Canadian Customs Department to learn if you may post a bond and/or other means to allow entry to their country. It just makes great sense to find out about the restrictions prior to arrival at the border crossing so you will not be turned away.

As a general rule, Canada <u>does not</u> allow individuals with a DUI conviction to enter their country. However, travelers who require in-depth information regarding the process of applying for a waiver or other admissibility questions can reach the Canada Border Services Agency (CBSA) during regular business hours, Monday to Friday (08:00 - 16:00 local time, except holidays) by calling either (506) 636-5064 or (204) 983-3500.

If you are not familiar with restricted items, that is, items not allowed in Canada, please do yourself a big favor and find out before you set out on the road. If you have firearms or ammunition with you, plan on the possibility of a lengthy delay as Canada requires all firearms to be registered, and they may put an official seal on your weapons. In the event you attempt to take a handgun into Canada, be aware that you are probably committing a crime.

Do not attempt to take items such as pepper spray or mace into Canada. Also, there are limitations with respect to the quantity of alcohol, (to include beer), cigarettes and cigars and other tobacco products. There may be seasonal restrictions with respect to certain types of fruits and vegetables and it is not recommended that you seek to take live plants of any kind into Canada.

Traveling in Canada

Canada Day. If you are traveling in Canada around the first of July, be aware that this is Canada Day, similar to the U.S. Fourth of July. As such, you may encounter RV parks that are full of holiday campers. So far in all of our travels, we have encountered conflicts with this holiday only one time.

Follow the Rules and the Laws. We have yet to encounter problems with the local police and/or the

Royal Mounted. Of course, we respect the speed limits. After so many miles/kilometers driven in our northern neighbor's land, we have no problem understanding and following the speed limits which are in kilometers. If you do not follow the speed limits, especially through the cities and towns, you will probably meet the cadre who are given the task of protecting the citizenry and enforcing the laws. You might also be aware, that in the event you are held for speeding and or other vehicle violations, in addition to a hefty fine you may find yourself detained for a lengthy period.

Currency and Credit Cards in Canada. Years ago, we exchanged American dollars for Canadian dollars and paid for all our expenses with the foreign money. Over the last few years we have found this to be non-productive, and we always wound up with excess Canadian dollars. We now pay for everything with credit cards. Visa and MasterCard are readily accepted almost everywhere, but Discover Card is accepted at very few places in Canada.

We suggest that you contact your credit card company(s) and let them know that you will be traveling extensively in the U.S., in Canada and Alaska. They may deny a transaction and try to contact you for verification of your purchase.

We have encountered, in the past, situations whereby one of our credit cards has been denied. In some cases we think this is a scam by a local merchant who wants cash payment rather than accept credit.

Another consideration that you should know about is paying for fuel at the pump. Many of the Canadian service stations have the pay-at-the-pump operation set to handle only Canadian issued credit cards. Therefore, you may have to go inside the service station prior to pumping the fuel. Don't get discouraged with this as you probably need the leg exercise anyway.

Cell Phone Use in Canada. It is probably safe to say that most everyone knows that access to cell phone usage in our Great Nation is almost universal. However, in some of the remote areas of the Great Plains, including Montana and Wyoming, there are still some blind spots. We have encountered only minor difficulties with cell phone usage as it seems almost every town, no matter how small, provides access.

Cell phone usage in Canada is the same as in the U.S. – tower coverage almost anywhere in and around the cities. However, in the remote areas one should not assume cell access will be available. In fact, one should assume that cell phone access WILL NOT be available in remote areas, and it is certainly very limited along the Alcan Highway. Also, it is our experience that the cost for roaming charges and usage in Canada can be rather expensive. Accordingly, we do not use our cell phones unless absolutely necessary. Right before we cross into Canada, we advise our family and friends not to expect any contact from us until we are in Alaska.

In addition to our cell phones we carry a Citizen's Band (CB) radio. Back in the heyday of CB trucker traffic there was a certain enjoyment to listen in and share some chuckles with the voices traveling up and down the highways. Sadly, it seems those days are now just a memory as most CB traffic is quite garbled and not worth the trouble. We use our CB for only two purposes: 1) as a means to find out why we are in the midst of a traffic jam (very, very seldom) and how long it may be until we get back on our way, and 2) the CB unit we have provides weather alert information. On those occasions when dark skies loom on the horizon, we turn to the weather channel to learn of any weather warnings. You will not want to venture into severe weather such as high winds and hail that could damage to your RV.

All of the weather advisories and warnings issued by the National Weather Service are specific to selected counties within a state. For us it is not easy to locate a specific county on our road maps – in fact, it is downright impossible. A few years ago we accessed the internet and made a copy of a map for each state we travel through showing only the counties. We keep these copies in our trailer and move them to the pickup when we head off on our next adventure.

<u>Wi-Fi Access in Canada</u>. Almost all RV parks in the U.S. now have Wi-Fi access. However, many of the RV parks have Wi-Fi which is only accessible from the office. The same is true of the RV parks in Canada. In the very remote areas along the Alcan

Highway, Wi-Fi access is probably non-existent.

For what it is worth, we found a Wi-Fi reception booster which plugs into one of the USB ports on the computer and requires no installation or downloading. The booster was not very expensive, and it does help with Wi-Fi reception.

To stay in touch with your family and friends while you are traveling through Canada you might restrict your communications to e-mail rather than paying the higher cost for roaming charges associated with cell phone usage.

<u>GPS, Sirius, and Commercial Radio in Canada</u>. Modern technology has blessed many of us with such innovations as sliced bread, microwave ovens, and even electric toothbrushes. The really modern folks may take advantage of "Buck Rogers inventions" (the geezer version of "Star Wars") such as a global positioning system (GPS). So far, we have eluded this nuisance to the pioneering spirit, but we are aware that it can be a significant tool.

If we understand how things work, one enters a destination, and the device monitors the left and right turns and "tells" which way to go. Because we do not have such a device, we cannot state for sure these things will work in the remote corners of British Columbia, the Yukon, and Alaska. However, your destination is Alaska and there is really only one road to follow – it will be difficult to miss.

We have had the pleasure of access to Sirius radio, but the reception deteriorates the farther north we travel. By the time we arrive in Fairbanks, the reception is sporadic. However, there are reports that this deflection of the satellite may be rectified in the near future. Without Sirius the possibility of receiving radio signals in the remote areas is just that: remote. However, around the larger cities in Canada BBC is always on the air.

The pavement is good over almost all of the Alcan Highway.

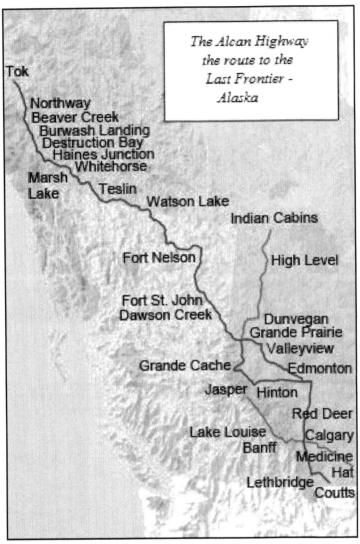

Map showing towns of interest from the Canadian Border to Tok, Alaska.

Travel around Calgary, Alberta. For those electing to take the route through Alberta, special attention should be made for travel around the large city of Calgary. First of all, it is recommended that you have sufficient fuel prior to entering the city proper. If you were to need fuel while traveling through Calgary it would be very difficult to find a service station and get back on the highway.

As you approach Calgary from the South pay special attention to the road signs directing you to the Deerfoot Trail. The signage identifying this thoroughfare is rather small compared to the large signs we are used to on the interstate system. As you come from Fort McLeod you will be on Highway 2. You will want to stay on this highway all the way to the north side of Calgary and on to Red Deer and beyond to Leduc. There are no stop signs on the Deerfoot Trail, but traffic is always heavy and special caution should be taken. We recommend you get in the center lane and stay there until you reach the north side of Calgary. For what it's worth, we try to set our itinerary to go through Calgary on a weekend.

Travel around Edmonton, Alberta. For many years we have totally avoided going through Edmonton. In the distant past it was an easy task. But now the city is so large that it is difficult to maneuver the RV through the many miles now encompassing this northern city with its never ending stop and go – well, we avoid those hours of frustration.

Traveling on Highway 2 from Calgary and through Red Deer, we continue north all the way to Leduc just south of Edmonton. To avoid Edmonton, we take Highway 39 west at Leduc and connect with Highway 60 (turning right) to the city of Devon. Beyond Devon, we continue north until we intersect with Highway 16 (avoid Highway 16 A, unless you want to drive through several towns and encounter lots of red and green lights.) We take Highway 16 west until we come to Highway 43 where we turn north heading for Whitecourt. The signage for Highway 43 and the Alcan Highway turn is clearly marked.

Traveling in Northwest Alberta. Driving north from Edmonton there is a significant reduction in traffic congestion. However, we advise to be extra cautious of the many large trucks. Also, take note that deer may be encountered in these semi-remote areas. We recommend that you do not tailgate other vehicles as your range of vision can be diminished.

The main towns of Whitecourt, Valleyview, and Grand Prairie offer full services, and most services can be obtained at the smaller cities of Onoway, Mayerthorpe, and Fox Creek.

Next stop – Dawson Creek, the start of the Alcan.

The Alcan Highway

When you have arrived at Dawson Creek, the start of the Alcan Highway, you're ready for the next phase of your great adventure. As most tourists do, you might want to have your picture taken beside the post which identifies mile zero of the Highway. Now it's time to head north to Alaska.

You may have heard horror stories describing the terrible conditions of the Highway – the need for extra tires, loads of spare gas, windshield and headlight protectors, and even undercarriage protection to avoid damage to oil pans, gas tanks, and mufflers.

If this is the case, you'll be pleasantly surprised not only with the first miles north of Dawson Creek, but all the way to the Alaskan border.

In this section we will seek to give you general information about the many facets of the Highway along with some specifics you may find helpful. Remember, we do not want to bore you nor do we wish to be a tour guide.

After leaving Dawson Creek, the next city you will come to is Taylor which is adjacent to Fort St. John. Of special note for the first-time traveler is the descent to the Peace River. If, in all your travels, you have never encountered a steep decline, then your initiation is about to begin. For sure there are many agencies and organizations that will provide instructions and recommendations on how to travel safely down steep hills. Suffice it to say you can't go wrong by going slow.

The steep decline to the Peace River and Taylor is one of several you'll encounter on the highway. We single this one out for your attention as it is the first serious descent you'll come to. Much further along the highway you will come to another of several "go downs" which can be treacherous for the uninitiated, especially if the weather is bad. Be careful when you come to the Sikanni River. We will not bore you with identifying each and every hill and decline along the highway. Suffice it to say, for those of you new to this type of roadway, by the time you pass the Sikanni River you should have sufficient experience for the rest of the trip.

Mechanical and Operational Considerations before You Go

Engines. We recommend a full service for your tow vehicle just prior to your departure. Most vehicles today will not require an oil change for at least 3,000 miles and many allow 5,000 miles between oil changes. Further, we recommend a FULL service to include brakes, battery, and transfer case. Check everything as recommended by the manufacturer.

Bearings – Trailer. We make the assumption that

you are not familiar with bearings. Accordingly, we strongly suggest that you find someone who can explain how bearings work and the causes for failures. Your RV dealer would be the first contact and their maintenance personnel should provide adequate instructions. Insist that your dealer provide you with a complete parts list identifying ALL parts which make up the bearing set. Also, you might go online to learn general information on the many facets of bearings.

Considering that you're going to be driving to and from Alaska, a distance of approximately 8,000 miles or more, we strongly recommend that you take a minimum of two complete sets of bearings for your RV – sufficient to replace bearings on two wheels. One complete set of bearings will probably not exceed $30 in cost. You may never need to use these spare bearings. However, it's a relatively inexpensive insurance.

Consider the unlikely possibility that you will have a bearing go bad out in the middle of the Yukon, forty miles from the nearest place of assistance. One way or another you make it to a facility where repairs can be made. However, you may sit there for several days waiting for parts to arrive from Edmonton or Chicago or Timbuktu. Murphy's Law dictates that the parts, when you receive them, will not be the correct parts or at least one item will be missing. Take extra bearings with you. Further, add some <u>high speed</u> grease and a grease gun. It is recommended that you squirt grease in each bearing every 1,000 miles. (Follow the directions provided by the RV manufacturer.)

A few years ago, after problems with bearings, we purchased a small, inexpensive "thermometer" to monitor the heat level of the bearings. We do this every time we stop for fuel and at each rest stop. It is a simple, non-time consuming task to walk around and hold the monitor right on the bearing casing. It is sort of like carrying an umbrella: carry one and it never rains.

In the event you are forced to replace bearings on your RV you will probably find that all goes well (providing you did your homework) until you come to fitting the dust cap – the last item to replace. It seems that every time we attempted, the cap would not go back on. To solve this problem, we purchased an inexpensive tool designed specifically for tapping on the dust covers.

Should you find that you are missing a dust cover, one can be fashioned from just about anything – cardboard, plastic bottle – and with just the right amount of duck tape you can easily make it to the next town.

Following are the basics of packing wheel bearings on a trailer with drum brakes.
- Jack up the axle and safely support it.
- Remove the wheel and tire.
- Remove the dust cap.
- Remove the cotter pin.
- Back the retaining nut off and wiggle the hub assembly to loosen the outer bearing on the axle.
- Remove the retaining nut, washer, and outer bearing.
- Slide the hub assembly off the axle stub.
- Clean the brake shoes, backing plate, and axle stub so they are ready for reassembly.
- Knock the inner bearing and grease seal out of the hub.
- Clean the brake dust from the brake drum, and the grease and dirt from the hub.

- Clean ALL, I repeat, ALL the old grease out of the bearings.

Now you should be ready for packing and re-assembly.

- Inspect the bearing races in the hub and put a light coating of grease on them.
- Hand pack grease into the bearings or pack using a bearing packing tool.
- Put the inner bearing into the hub. Install a new grease seal.
- Put a very thin coating of grease on the lip of the seal.
- Carefully slide the hub assembly onto the axle shaft, taking care not to damage the seal.
- Slide the outer bearing onto the axle stub, then the washer, and thread on the retaining nut.
- Tighten the retaining nut while rotating the drum taking all the slack out.
- Back the nut off and set the preload with a torque wrench.
- Install a new cotter pin.

- Replace the dust cap.
- Adjust the brakes.
- Repeat on the remaining wheels.

Follow all recommendations as prescribed by your manufacturer's specification, including proper torque amount and brake adjustment(s). We strongly suggest everyone become familiar with how bearings work and the exact way they are assembled. You should request maximum information from your RV dealer or a company that specializes in selling bearings. Request an "exploding view" which shows clearly how the bearings are assembled and defines each part. For example, the term "race" may be unfamiliar to many of you, but it is vital for the bearing to be assembled correctly.

Tires. Start your trip with good tires and a good spare. The cost of tires continues to climb higher and higher, seemingly every month. But consider the cost of a tire purchased in your hometown as opposed to the cost of a tire you must have. And when you need that tire, if it is available, you can bet it's going to be significantly more expensive in places like Fort Nelson, Whitehorse, or Haines

Junction.

You will travel over 8,000 miles on your trip. The blowout of one tire can ruin your adventure and cause serious damage. While the road conditions on the Alcan are very good in most places, there will probably be a few areas under construction. It is just a matter of common sense: don't start out with worn tires.

We advise you to take special notice of the tire wear on your trailer. Check all four tires with special attention to the inside edges. If there is uneven wear this may indicate the wheels are out of alignment, the axles are bent, or the camber[1] needs adjustment.

In addition to a good inspection of your tow vehicle tires, check the condition of the tires on your RV. Too often we tend to glance at the portions we can see easily. Before you set out on any trip, bend

---

[1] Camber angle is the angle made by the wheels of a vehicle. Specifically, it is the angle between the vertical axis of the wheels used for steering and the vertical axis of the vehicle when viewed from the front or rear. It is used in the design of steering and suspension. If the top of the wheel is farther out than the bottom (that is, away from the axle), it is called positive camber. If the bottom of the wheel is farther out than the top, it is called negative camber.

those knees and check the wear on the inside of the tires. If there is any wear at all, it may be possible you have a bent axle or the camber is out of alignment.

In most cities of any size there will be a trailer-truck re-conditioning company that specializes in solving these types of problems. Our experience proves the cost for inspection and repairs (if necessary) is minimal when compared to the cost of replacement of tires and the damage caused by a blowout. We take our trailer in for an annual inspection.

Tire pressure monitors. A few years ago we obtained pressure monitors for the tires on our RV. These are simple devices that screw onto the valve stems, one for each of the four tires. There is a battery inside each device which sends a signal to a monitor in our pickup cab which sounds an alarm if a tire should deflate below a certain pressure.

We highly recommend the use of these pressure monitors for all RV travel, but especially for travel on the Alcan. Consider you will leave your campsite in the morning, with your tow vehicle full of fuel, and you may drive for two or three hours without stopping again. During such time you may in fact be driving with a flat or blown tire and be totally unaware of it. The same thing could happen in the Lower Forty-Eight but you may be closer to assistance than on the Alcan. Consider that you may be traveling at say 55 mph with all the weight of your RV held by only one tire on a side.

<u>Brakes – Plus Controller</u>. If you do not have experience with brakes on an RV trailer or fifth wheel it is imperative that you become totally familiar with the operations and safety features involved. The purchase of an RV trailer must include detailed information with respect to the function, wear, and maintenance of the brakes installed on the trailer. Don't be a "know it all" or be ill at ease in seeking assistance from your dealership and their personnel.

Special attention is required for your safety with respect to the proper setting and necessary adjustments, if any, to ensure that the brake controller is functioning properly. Many of the later model pickups have a factory installed brake controller complete with the necessary wiring and adapters for hooking up your trailer. However, if your tow vehicle is not factory equipped, you will need to install a brake controller and possibly electrical wiring to operate the lights on the trailer.

Make sure that you are thoroughly familiar with the operations of the brake controller before you drive off from your dealership.

Hitch. The type of hitch you will need is dependent upon not only the type of vehicle you use as your tow vehicle but also the weight and type of RV trailer you are pulling. Your dealership should know what is required, and they should be more than willing to assist you to ensure the proper hitch is installed and meets all safety requirements.

Almost every RV trailer of any size will require anti-sway bars as part of the hitch. Special attention should be made with respect to the procedures in hooking the trailer to the tow vehicle as well as the procedures to unhook the RV. Remember, an extra thirty seconds of safety may prevent a disaster.

Power hitch. All three of our travel trailers had a power lift on the tongue to make it easier to hook to the tow vehicle. If you're looking for a new travel trailer be sure the dealer will provide a power lift. Also, make sure that the salesman or the maintenance personnel fully explains all the ins and outs of the proper method of attaching the anti-sway bars. We suggest you watch them hitch and unhitch at least twice. And then have them watch you do it. Be absolutely sure of the procedures before you drive off – take notes and write things down if you have to.

Using propane while driving. This subject could be covered very simply: **DON'T DO IT!**

There are some who will tell you that you can drive down the road with your propane tank on, supplying fuel to your refrigerator. They say this allows your food and beverages to remain cold and nothing will spoil. Take it from one who has seen several vehicles on the side of the road partially burned or completely blown apart by a propane explosion.

We have been traveling with our RVs on many roads, under many conditions, to include hundred degree Fahrenheit temperatures. We have yet to encounter spoilage of any kind in our refrigerator. We make it an absolute rule to remove anything we think we will need during the day from the refrigerator and place these items in a small cooler which goes in the truck with us.

Black water drain. Let's talk candidly about the black water tank. Almost all RV campgrounds, and even many rest stops along the interstate highways, have waste disposal facilities. This is really good news because it allows easy access to dispose of wastes.

Many RV parks and other locations have dumping stations. You might consider disposing of your black and grey water whenever the tanks are one-third full. Why carry the extra weight?

Bumper add-ons. There seems to be a new trend in many of the RVs that we have seen recently where various items can be stored (carried) at the exterior rear of the RV. At first glance, this appears to be a good way to take along bicycles, extra gas cans, etc. However, you should be sure that the bracing is adequate in stability as well as strength. We have heard of horror stories in which individuals have arrived at their destination only to find out that a motorized wheelchair did not make the whole trip.

Level braces – Power a plus and blocks. The current travel trailer that we have is equipped with motorized braces which may be operated by means of a remote control wireless device. Our first thought was that we would never use this. However, considering our age and the daily visits by Arthur Itis, it sure is nice to just push a button and have these braces extend.

We did make an addition to the system by placing blocks of wood cut from four by fours, underneath each brace. By so doing, the braces do not come down as far and therefore provide better stability for our trailer. One added little tip: attach a string to each block of wood so it's easier to remove them when you are ready to get back on the road.

Window Seals. Before you drive off the lot with your brand-new RV, travel trailer, pop-up, fifth wheel, or any other type of RV, make sure your windows do not leak. We believe there must be some law of nature that prescribes no rain for days prior to your driving off with your new purchase. Be sure to instruct your RV dealership to spray every window with a garden hose from several angles to ensure rainwater will not come in. You don't want to be at your destination or travel down the highways with rainwater seeping in and ruining the interior of your brand-new RV.

<u>Fresh Water</u>. We recommend a thorough cleaning of your fresh water tank before you go. Follow the manufacturer's recommendations or visit your local RV sales and service store – they will provide information on how to sanitize as well as the chemicals to keep your fresh water pure.

There is no need to fill your tank to the top. Fresh water is available at almost every stop along the way. We depart with our tank approximately one-third full.

You should equip your city water intake with a special valve that reduces water pressure to a rate low enough so that the PVC pipes will not burst. This valve should be a part of the package when you buy a new RV.

Another minor piece of advice: find out as much as you can about the water piping in your RV. It might be significantly helpful to know in advance where the access panels are to allow repairs to faucets and drains.

Hot Water Heater. Assuming you are relatively new to this great world of RVing, you might check the anode (heating element) in your water heater. The anode rod reduces the amount of corrosion in the hot water tank. During lengthy periods of non-operation (winter) the water heater should be drained. Overlooking this task may result in deterioration of the anode (heating element). It is a simple task with the proper tool to remove the element, inspect for deterioration and replace if necessary.

Essentials. Most RVs have storage space accessible from the exterior. Take a few moments and consider all the items you want to take along and just how valuable they are. Take into account how much weight you are placing in your RV. Following is a list of what we consider essentials:
- Air compressor (small type that plugs into power point)

- Batteries (supply of AA, AAA and at least one 9-volt)
- Fan (small oscillating type in case power for AC is not available)
- Small vacuum (we are gone a long time)
- One extra fresh water hose (may need for distance to spigot)
- Extra water hose gaskets
- Duct tape
- Drop cloth (old shower curtain)
- Work gloves
- Hand cleaner
- Towels and rags
- Heavy duty tow strap[2]
- WD-40 (good for windows)
- 50ft of heavy duty electric extension cord
- Miscellaneous electrical adaptors (hook-up to 15 or 30-amp)
- Brake/bearing cleaner (two spray cans)
- Assortment of small tools

---

[2] **Tow Strap** Most RVs are equipped with leaf-spring suspension. We reiterate that the Alcan Highway is paved and the chances of breaking a spring are remote, we recommend that you be prepared – just in case. Before you depart, visit a local company that deals with suspensions. Specifically, you want to know what to do in case a leaf spring breaks. In many situations, it is possible to tie back the axle with a tow strap so you can limp to the nearest facility for repairs.

- Leveling boards (two each - 2" x 6" slanted on one end)
- Two complete sets of spare wheel bearings
- Grease gun with high speed bearing grease

<u>Safety</u>. Every RV has (should have) at least one fire extinguisher generally located close to an exit door. It is recommended that you check to make sure you have a fire extinguisher and that it is in working condition.

In addition to the fire extinguisher in our travel trailer, we keep another one in our pickup in a location where we have immediate access to it. By so doing we can grab the extinguisher in an emergency without fumbling for keys to unlock the door to the trailer.

In the event you are required to back up in tight places (and you will), for maximum safety be sure to have someone outside of your rig to guide you.

Be sure your RV is equipped with workable smoke and CO_2 detectors – start off with new batteries.

Never drive off with the propane valves open.

Check the umbilical connection after every stop.

Electricity Hook-up. There are many gadgets and couplings available for a multitude of electrical hook-ups. We are speaking specifically of electrical hook-ups at an RV park. Most RVs today will use a standard 30-amp receptacle, and most RV parks are set up to accommodate just about any circumstance. The larger RVs, such as the Class A and some of the fifth wheels require a 50-amp service. Be aware that on the Alcan Highway most RV parks will be able to provide full hook-ups. In the event you require 50-amp services, remember that for most of the year, if not all the year, air-conditioning will not be required.

We carry with us an adapter whereby our standard 30-amp male plug can be converted to fit the normal 15-amp socket. In recent years we have rarely needed to use this, but it is sure nice to have should the situation ever require it. To be extra sure the RV park does in fact have 30-amp service, most RV parts and service outlets sell an inexpensive tester.

A small but very important tip: after your trailer is hooked up to your tow vehicle and the safety chains are in place and you hook up the umbilical cord (electrical connection from RV to tow vehicle) take a piece of duct tape and secure the receptacle so it will not accidentally come loose. Some years ago a trucker advised that we did not have any lights on our travel trailer. Taking a look around, we found the umbilical cord dragging on the pavement. Needless to say, it was a real hassle to fix the problem. More than likely, the cord was disengaged by vibration or someone stepping over the hitch and dragging a toe on the cord. From then on we have always taped the cord to the receptacle.

Fuses. Another thing before you leave the dealership: make sure you know where the fuse box is located, and we suggest you take along extra fuses. It is highly unlikely that you will encounter electrical problems during your trip. However, Murphy's Law dictates that if you need a fuse it will not be available. Also, make sure you know where the fuses are for all operations, including fuses not located in the standard fuse box. Make special note of fuse location(s) for the operation of the slides. We suggest you write down where the fuse boxes are located – don't rely on your memory.

TV operations. Some of you may think it strange that we have made a special mention of TV operations. However, based upon our experiences, when you have traveled for a full day and wish to relax with the news or your favorite program, you may find significant frustration in trying to operate your TV.

We strongly suggest that you spend extra time with your RV dealer going over all the procedures for your entertainment center to include hooking up to cable and/or satellite. We are not sure who writes the instructions for operating a TV, but we suspect they have a diabolical hatred for people such as us. Again, write it down.

Extra level blocks. Almost every RV park you encounter will have level parking spaces. However, you may wish to "tweak" your resting place just a bit. We carry four lengths of two-by-six treated wood which allows for leveling the trailer in just about any circumstances. There are several types of leveling blocks available at many of the RV parts and service stores.

We also add to our storage compartments four

blocks of wood four-by-four by-twelve (high) which we place directly under the stabilizing braces. By so doing, we achieve significantly greater stability.

Other Tips and Suggestions

<u>Diary</u>. You might consider keeping a diary of your trip – both to and from the Great Land. How often have you heard: "I wish we had kept a diary," or "I wish we had a video?" Today's technology provides for many inexpensive, hand-held recorders and one might even be able to voice record to an iPad or tablet. The point to be made is: this may be your once in a lifetime trip, and you will want to share your adventures with friends and relatives. We suggest you "write it down" and "get it in writing," so you have it to recall when you send out next year's Christmas letter.

<u>Some Other Items to Take Along</u>. Perhaps the only area where disagreements may occur is the need to take everything along. First of all, always take into consideration how much weight you are adding. Make sure you do not overload your RV's maximum weight limits as well as keeping a balanced load. Also, added weight in your RV or in your tow vehicle will ultimately have an affect on your fuel mileage.

We don't argue anymore about what to take – Gloria is the Boss. However, we do take care with respect to our weight limit. There is a tendency to stock up on food provisions, especially with canned goods such as soups, beans, etc. Perhaps it is good to mention that there are many supermarkets along the way, and the prices for many items will not be out-of-line in Fairbanks or Anchorage. We suggest taking two or three cans of soup to consume along the way and then re-stock as required.

However, we should caution that some items may be significantly higher in Canada. For instance, we have found the price of milk to be as much as double what we pay for it in the Lower Forty-Eight. So, we buy our milk just before we cross over into Canada. Also on the high-priced list are snacks such as chips, nuts, and cereals. These items have virtually no weight to them, and we take along a bountiful collection.

There are many stories still in circulation which describe the Alcan as a virtual wasteland of wrecked and abandoned vehicles brought about by terrible road conditions. Let's put the record straight: the Alcan is a very good road, paved most of the way and with only small portions in need of repair. Fuel and services are readily available. Up until the time the Alcan was paved, many RV parks were not developed for lack of traffic, and there were significant stretches where available services were in short supply. Those days of horrendous travel conditions are found in the pages of history.

Considering the foregoing, there is no critical need to take extra tires and extra gas. Start off with good (preferably new) tires that will bring you safely home after 8,000 plus miles. Watch your fuel gauge and fill up more often than you might normally do. If you have the means to safely secure a fuel can on the outside of your rig, you might consider doing so. There is a long stretch before you reach Watson Lake where the price of fuel can be quite high. An extra five gallons just may come in handy.

Take along an extra jacket, sweater or sweatshirt

to ward off the chills in the Canadian Rockies. Add a pair of work gloves in case you need to change a tire and a drop cloth (an old shower curtain) in case Murphy's Law prevails and a flat tire occurs just where the mud puddles are. We always take along a small container of hand cleaner such as "Fast Orange" or "GOJO" and a supply of disposable rags or towels. At every fuel stop we make sure we clean the windshield to rid the glass of the insect graveyard. In addition, we take along a bottle of Windex and clean the glass every morning before we set out for the day.

An absolute necessity is insect repellent. There are many folks who will use nothing but Off. For us, we have found that Cutter's is superior. No matter what your preference, be sure to bring some along. In Alaska you might consider buying or renting a shotgun – in case the larger mosquitoes come after you.

In addition to mosquitoes, there are "no-see-ums" which may leave a welt about the size of a dime and stay with you for two or three weeks. The worst is the evil "white socks." These little monsters burrow so deep, the only thing sticking out of your skin are the white socks. For small children we recommend some type of hat to ward off the possibility of horse flies, also known as breeze flies, clegs, klegs, or clags, deer flies, gadflies, or zimbs. In some areas of Canada, they also are known as bulldog flies.

We have found the most convenient dispersal to be the finger-pump type spray. This is easier and safer to transfer the spray from hand to forehead and neck areas, and there is less chance of leakage from the container.

Consider taking a small oscillating fan in case you stay where the electricity source does not support your A/C. Also, we have found that in most places in British Columbia, the Yukon, and Alaska we are comfortable with just a fan and we do not have to listen to the roar of the A/C. We love the fresh air coming through the open windows and doors.

Checklist. For those of you who are "ancients" when it comes to the world of RVing, you probably don't need a checklist – it's the same as breathing these days. For the newly initiated, we recommend a checklist of important things to do before departing for the next destination.

We will pass over the obvious things to take care of inside the trailer – dishes, cabinet doors, etc. However, before you bring in your slide(s) make sure there are no obstacles in the path. Turn off your refrigerator, outside lights, water pump, and anything else that might drain the battery on your RV. If you have a pet, it is best to pour out the water dish – no need to slosh all over the floor.

Close the ceiling air vents, turn off the fans, and, perhaps the most overlooked of all – retract the TV antennae.

We do two walk-arounds before we head out for the day. The first is an inspection to see if there are any problems: water leaks, tire condition, etc. The second outside tour is made to ensure all the following necessities have been taken care of:

- Water line disconnected and stored
- Electricity cable disconnected and stored
- Cable TV hook-up disconnected and stored
- Wheel blocks removed and stored
- Stabilizer jack retracted
- Steps in storage position

- Storage compartments closed and locked
- All windows shut
- Propane cylinders turned off
- Propane covers and lid in place
- Antennae in traveling position (on roof)

When all is ready, we start the tow vehicle (diesel) and idle for a maximum of five minutes. Letting your vehicle idle more than five minutes is probably doing more harm than good. Check your manufacturer's recommendations.

Our final checklist ensures we have all the children, dogs, vagrants, owls, and any other creature that might be with us. So far we have not left anyone or anything behind – that we know of or will admit to.

<u>Propane Tank Cover</u>. All RVs today have propane tanks with a cover. Most have small eyelets on the bottom to place tie-downs. We use a bungee cord. We lost a cover in a windstorm before we knew of this. Also, our propane cover has a hinged plate which allows for access to the valves without removing the entire cover – good idea. However, we have found over time that the hinge may wear out.

To make sure we do not lose this plate, we drilled small holes in both the plate and the cover and installed zip-strip connectors.

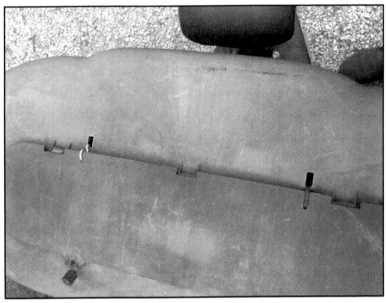

Our propane tank cover showing the zip-tie connectors ensuring that the cover stays together in case of hinge failure.

Walk-around Inspection. Before you depart for the lands of the north, do a walk around inspection of your RV. Some of those screw heads with the square nib on the head may need to be tightened. Check for separations in caulking and pay special attention to any areas where the caulk may have deteriorated to the point that water can pass through.

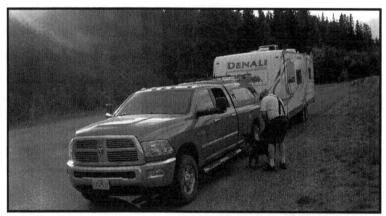

The habit of doing a walk-around when you stop for a break, gas, or food can save you from a mishap. Even our dog Rocky tags along for the look-over.

Mileage and Facilities

During our annual trip in 2013, we made note of the mileage between places. In the table following, you will find the bare outline of that task. Please note that the mileage as we recorded it may not be the same as the historical miles due to significant changes brought about by the modernization of the Alcan. However, our numbers are within acceptable accuracy, and this will give you approximate distances.

We also make note of services which may or may not be available. There is no way we can guarantee that you will find the services to be as we make note. Further, we do not make any attempt to promote by favor or disfavor any facility. If we have excluded any facility such omission would be strictly due to oversight.

RVing North to Alaska

Table of RV Parks and a Few Points of Interest.

Point of Interest	Mile	Facilities
Dawson Creek	0	Full Services – RV Park
Taylor	34	Full Services – RV Park
Ft. St. John	44	Full Services – RV Park
Charlie Lake	50	Full Services – RV Park
Shepherd Inn	73	
Wonowon	102	Fuel - ?? RV Park
Pink Mountain	142	Fuel - Restaurant
Sasquatch Crossing	145	?? Fuel -- ?? RV Park
Sikanni Chief	160	Cabins -- ?? RV Park
Buckinghorse River	175	
Prophet River	228	
Ft. Nelson	278	Full Services
Steamboat Mountain	335	
Tetsa River 1	344	Campground
Tetsa River 2	354	?? RV Park
Stone Mtn. Provincial Park	371	Provincial Park
Rocky Mountain Lodge	376	Closed
Toad River	402	Fuel -- RV Park
Poplar's RV/Camp	404	Cabins – dry camp
Muncho Lake Prov. Park	435	Provincial Park
Double G Services	433	?? Closed
Strawberry Flats	434	Campground
North. Rockies Lodge	440	?? RV Park
Muncho Lake RV Park	435	Closed
Laird River Hot Springs	475	Fuel -- RV Park
Laird River Provincial Park	475	Provincial Park
Coal River RV	511	RV Park -- ?? Fuel
Fireside	520	Closed
Contact Creek	562	
Iron Creek	568	Closed
Watson Lake	600	Full Services
Upper Laird	611	Closed

Junction 37 Services	618	Fuel -- Cabins
Big Creek Campground	642	Closed
Rancheria	678	RV Park
Continental Divide	689	Rest - RV Park
Swift River	701	Closed
Marley River	743	Closed
Dawson Peaks	759	Closed
Teslin	761	Fuel - RV Park
Mukluk Annie's	775	Closed
Timberpoint Campground	787	Campground
Johnson Crossing	798	?? RV Park -- ?? Fuel
Seguenda Lake	810	?? Campground
Jake's Corner	826	Fuel Rest /Bakery
Marsh Lake Campground	849	Closed
Caribou RV Services	864	RV Park
Whitehorse	865	Full Services
Otter Falls Cut Off	952	RV Park - Rest
Pine Lake Campground	968	Campground
Haines Jct.	972	Full Services
Cottonwood RV Park	1021	Closed
Condon Creek	1026	Campground
Destruction Bay	1037	Fuel-RV Park-Rest
Burwash Landing	1047	?? RV Park
Kluane Wilderness Village	1070	
Pine Valley	1099	Closed
Lake Creek Campground	1104	Campground
Koidern	1114	?? Closed
Bear Flats	1119	Closed
White River RV Park	1120	RV Park -- ?? Fuel
Beaver Creek	1167	Full Services
Border City	1177	Fuel-RV Park

Highlights along the Way

The Alcan Highway, whether you use the official name Alaska Highway or the Alaskan-Canadian Highway, holds a mystique for those who seek adventure. There are those who respond to the question "Why climb mountains?" with the answer "Because it is there." For those who seek to travel the Alcan the answer might be "To see the beauty of God's handiwork."

Beginning at Dawson Creek, British Columbia and ending at Fairbanks, Alaska, the total length is 1,488 miles (2,394 km). Now there are some who claim that the official ending of the Alcan is located at Delta Junction in Alaska where it joins with the Richardson Highway. Technically, they have a point as there was a road of sorts from Fairbanks to Valdez (pronounced Val-deeez) named the Richardson

Highway. However, one should consider that the Alcan was not built to get to Delta Junction – it was built to reach Fairbanks.

Today the Highway is significantly different than it was when completed in 1942. We now have pavement all the way even though a few stretches will be under annual maintenance. The road is excellent except for the frost heaves in the far northwestern parts of the Yukon. Many sections exceed the quality of some highways in the lower 48. However, there are sections which require extreme caution due to narrow lanes, sharp bends with restricted vision, the presence of wildlife, and steep grades. The prudent driver will encounter all that the Alcan has to offer and then brag, or even lie, to the grandchildren of his exploits.

In the following pages we identify RV parks at specific locations. This information is provided as a helpful means to make your trip more enjoyable and less stressful. We cannot guarantee that these facilities will be operating during any given time. Some are open only during the summer months and some may not provide full services throughout the year. Further, we are guarded when it comes to recommendations. The facilities we consider adequate may fall short of the expectations of others.

The Alcan starts at Dawson Creek. However, your adventure begins when you decide to go "because it is there" and you want to experience "the beauty of God's handiwork." So, how to define a starting point – when you close your front door, pull out of the driveway and inch onto the highway? Maybe it is best to keep in mind that you are on your "RV Trip of a Lifetime." It is within your reach to explore all the great things to see and do from your home all the way to Edmonton on short trips – save these destinations for future trips. We think in terms of obtaining the first door to a wilderness which is for us those reaches beyond Edmonton.

Edmonton to Dawson Creek

You leave the environs of the last large metropolis – Edmonton – and seek a sign which beckons: "Alaska, turn right." From here the congestion fades in the rear view mirrors. The vista is widespread, but remoteness gradually begins to seep on the horizon. You look for other RVs, straining to obtain the location of their homes by the license plates. Are they going north? No, that rig is local, somewhere here in Alberta.

Onoway is the first town, but it is set back from the highway, so you continue on to Mayerthorpe, easing back on the throttle seeking that relaxing shift of the body melding into your seat. Yes, there are miles yet to travel before reaching Dawson Creek, but the scenery is open, the roadway is smooth, and all that traffic is left behind.

Mayerthorpe is a small town with lots of services but no RV park that we know of. Continue on to Whitecourt which has full facilities and services. There are two RV parks: one is operated by the

Lions Club and is located on the left side as you approach the city. The other RV park, **Sagitawa**, is located on the west side of the city (exit to the right.) This RV park has maintained an almost full capacity over the past few years. In 2012, we secured the last available spot. Also, the pull-through spaces are not slanted. Thus, if you have minimal experience maneuvering your rig into tight spaces, you might want to consider the **Lions RV Park.**

The next town you'll come to is Fox Creek, a very new community which appears to have full services for the RV tourists. **Fox Creek RV Park and Campground** has full hook-ups. It is our understanding that reservations are not taken. There are two campgrounds within ten miles, but neither has electricity or water. We have never stayed at this town, so we are unable to comment further. Depending upon our length of travel for the day, we spend the night at Whitecourt or travel on to Valleyview which is another full-service community.

There are two RV parks in Valleyview:

Sands Wilderness, which is situated along Highway 43, provides water, electricity, showers, and laundry. It has 49 campsites.

Sherk's RV Park is one-half mile west of Valleyview. There are full hook-ups at all stalls, 42 back-in and 14 pull-through sites, 24-hour security, laundry facilities, showers, and a playground. We have stayed at **Sherk'**s almost too many times to count. This is without a doubt one of the best managed RV parks we have encountered.

As you travel on to Grand Prairie, past Bezanson, look to the right of the road where you might see elk, buffalo, or caribou in research enclosures. Grand Prairie is a very large city with all services. There are many RV parks in the Grand Prairie area, but we have never stopped for a night here.

Country Roads RV Park – A Good Sam Park. To find it, stop and ask for directions.

Legion Park. There is probably no electricity or water here.

Camp Tamarack RV Park Inc. – A Good Sam Park. It is located 5 miles south of the junction of Highways 43 and 40.

Stampede Campground and RV Park – It is located on the north side of Highway 43, just west of the intersection of 100 Avenue and 108th Street – just west of Riocan Grand Prairie Center.

Nitehawk Rotary RV Park – A Good Sam Park
Directions: From the junction of Highways 43 and 40, go south 11.6km/7.2 miles on Highway 40 to Highway 666 (Nitehawk Exit), then go west 3.9km/2.4 miles to Nitehawk Ski Hill.

Grande Prairie Rotary RV Park
Directions: From the junction of Highways 40 and 43 (108 St.), go north 77 yds/70 m on Highway 43, then east 30 yds/27m on 107 Avenue, then north 140 yds/128m on the frontage road.

Directions for travelling through Grand Prairie are well marked, it is best to stay in the right hand lane(s) as the route to Alaska requires all turns to the right.

West of Grand Prairie the terrain changes slightly with rolling hills, but the road continues in long straight stretches. The next town is Beaver Lodge which does have an RV park. **Beaverlodge Pioneer Campground,** located on the west side of town, has 29 stalls and 10 full-service sites. The price of admission includes water and firewood.

The next town is Hythe which also has an RV park: **Hythe Municipal Campground.** This RV park does not have 50-amp service nor do they provide pull-through sites.

The last city you will encounter before Dawson Creek is Pouce Coupe (we don't know how to pronounce it either). We do caution you to drive within the speed limits through Pouce Coupe.

Dawson Creek to Fort Nelson

Just a short distance up the road is Dawson Creek, the beginning of the Alcan. Travel through the city is not difficult. As you go around the circle heading for Highway 97, you might want to stop at the tourist information facility which has an excellent parking area for RVs. Also, while parked there, you can visit the town and have pictures taken at the Mile Post 0 Marker (most tourists do). Note that you are now in British Columbia, and there is a time change to Mountain Time.

There are several RV parks located in the Dawson Creek area – ask at the tourist information center for directions.

Alahart RV & Tent Park
Farmington Fairways RV Resort
Mile 0 Campground – A Good Sam Park
Northern Lights RV Park
Tubby's RV Park

Milepost 0 in downtown Dawson Creek.

Perhaps you spent a night where the Alcan begins. It is a good place to rest before the great adventure gets underway. Now you are actually on the road – the Alcan. The terrain is not that much different, but the scenery seems to be a bit more remote. As you leave Dawson Creek, you leave the divided highway behind. If you need to pass another vehicle, do so with caution. Watch especially for trucks turning onto the highway and don't forget to keep an eye out for the wildlife on the road.

Just up the road a ways you'll be coming to the Peace River. If you have not been here before, note that the Peace River eventually flows into the Arctic Ocean by way of the MacKenzie River. Do you feel you have arrived in the North Country? Before you begin the descent to the Peace River and to the city of Taylor, there is a pull-off where trucks must stop to check their brakes. If you need a rest or need to check your brakes, be sure to do so before heading on. The descent is steep, possibly the steepest you have ever encountered. Be sure to use extreme caution.

Just across the Peace River is Taylor with Fort St. John just 18 miles further. Both municipalities have full services with Fort St. John offering considerably more for the tourist. Taylor offers two RV parks:

Peace Island Regional Park Campground is located at the bottom of the hill right before you cross the river, and **Fairway RV Park** is located on the left side of the highway approximately three-fourths of a mile from the bridge.

On the west side of Taylor, the road winds and climbs steeply up to the plateau and on to Fort St. John. For what it's worth, we always obtain fuel before leaving the city. There are two RV parks: **Ross H. Maclean Rotary RV Park,** located just six miles north of downtown Fort St. John, and **Charlie Lake RV & Leisure**, which is located on the west side of Fort St. John. It is easily seen from the highway. Before leaving Charlie Lake, you might want to check the weather report. You can ask a southbound trucker or the sales clerk at the gas station. If your travel is in the early spring (May) there is a chance, even if remote, that bad weather might be ahead.

Between Charlie Lake (Fort St. John area) and Fort Nelson, a distance of 230 miles, there are several roadside businesses that provide fuel, lodging, restaurant, and RV parks. The first such stop is **Shepherd's Inn**, which has a motel, restaurant, fuel, and an RV park. Next is the town of Wonowon, so called because of the phonetic sound of "Mile 101." There are minimal facilities, but fuel and motel accommodations are available. Gradually you will be climbing to Pink Mountain, so named because at certain times, especially in the dawn's light, the hills take on a pinkish tint due to the blossoms of the fireweed. There is an advertised RV park and a fuel station. However, we have never spent a night here and have not required fuel.

Four miles further on is the roadside stop of **Sasquatch Crossing**. We have seen a lot of things cross the road over the many years we have traveled on the Alcan. However, we have yet to see the namesake of this area – but we do keep our eyes open. This stop, which is also known as **Sportsman's Inn,** has fuel, a motel, and an RV park. In this area, on a clear day you can see the Canadian Rockies.

From the highest point in this section of the Alcan, at Pink Mountain, you will begin the descent to the Sikanni River. The road leading to the river is very steep, and you must take care, adjust your speed, and take it slow. At the bottom of the hill is the **Sikanni Chief Campground and RV Park,** which advertises full RV services, including fuel.

At Mile 173, **Buckinghorse River Lodge** advertises free RV parking **without** hook-ups, a restaurant, fuel and propane. However, we question whether this facility is open year-round. The **Buckinghorse River Wayside Provincial Park** is open from May 1 through September 1. It provides full-service RV hook-ups. From this location it is approximately 110 miles to Fort Nelson. There is one roadside stop at Prophet River that provides minimal, if any, services.

The city of Fort Nelson has a history which dates back to the Hudson Bay Trading Post. First established in 1804, the community remained a small outpost until 1942 when the construction of the Alcan began. A minor note of history states that an alternate route to the Alcan was built in the event of Japanese attack on the Alcan Highway. This alternate route leads to Fort Simpson and is known as the Fort Simpson, Mackenzie River Route. Today, Fort Nelson is a large city with full services.

For the RV traveler, in Fort Nelson there are two RV parks: **Triple "G" Hideaway RV Park & Restaurant**, another Good Sam RV park which is open all year with full hook ups (maximum 30-amp service) located on the west or north side of town and the **Blue Bell Inn RV**, located in town. This RV park has only eight pull-throughs.

Before you leave the Fort Nelson area, we strongly suggest you fill up with fuel. There are places to obtain fuel between Fort Nelson and the next large town, Watson Lake (approximately 300 miles.) However, prices for fuel may be considerably higher in the remote areas.

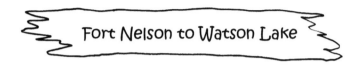
Fort Nelson to Watson Lake

So far in your adventure, you have encountered minimal grandeur in the passing scenery. Hopefully you will have seen some of the wildlife, and the weather has been in your favor. As you depart Fort Nelson, the scenery will turn spectacular!

Gradually you will climb in elevation to an area known as Steamboat Mountain. You will not actually be on the mountain as it is several miles to the northeast, but you will have ample places to pull off and take in the vastness spilled to the horizon and beyond. The road is considerably less steep than other "slow-me-downs," but we still advise caution – make sure you do not overheat your brakes.

On this stretch of the Alcan the services are somewhat few and far between. There are facilities at Tetsa River 1 and Tetsa River 2 but to our knowledge there are no hook-ups for electricity or water.

By the time you arrive at Stone Mountain Provincial Park, you may not believe the scenery can get any better. Just you wait. As Al Jolson was famous for saying, "You ain't seen nothin' yet!"

The road then begins to wind, and all those straight stretches are far behind. You climb some hills and then some more hills and eventually you see the remnants of Summit Lodge on your left. Just past here is **Summit Lake Provincial Park**, right off the highway and right at the water's edge. There is a pull-off to the right if you wish to stop for pictures. The park is open on a first-come first-serve basis, but there is no electricity or water service for RVs.

The distance to the next RV park may seem like a long way, but the scenery is worth the time. The Alcan seems to meander for a while, taking you on top of several crests, and then plunges down, steeply. All the while, the mountains reflect the brilliance – all that nature can provide. There are bighorn sheep and caribou right in the middle of the road, and if one is going too fast a vacation can be ruined in a heartbeat. The gradient is steep, but everyone is enthralled with the Canadian Rockies. So, going slow is tolerated and encouraged. There are ample pull-offs for sightseeing and picture taking. Take care not to block the path of the large trucks – they may not be able to stop in a short space.

The end of the decline finds you just a few miles from **Toad River Lodge**, located at Mile 422. It offers cabins, a restaurant, and full hook-ups for the RV traveler. Fuel may be available but be prepared for high prices. Also, consider that the next available place to obtain fuel will be just as high and Watson Lake in the Yukon is still 200 miles away. It would be great if we could offer some advice as to the lowest prices for fuel, but such is not the case.

Just a short way further on is **Poplar's Camping and RV Park**. This facility is operated by the Clements family who we hold as close friends. The restaurant has been closed since 2010 but there are cabins. The RV park may or may not be open for individual tourists. It is our understanding that Poplar's is open to RV caravans. They do provide camping/tenting and may provide RV dry camping.

As you continue on from this area, be mindful of the wildlife on the road. We have encountered deer, elk, moose, and bear. Hopefully you will see many creatures but take care not to run into one. The scenery continues to be spectacular with high, snow-clad mountains and winding roads alongside the many rivers. Each turn in the road brings a new vista.

You can see a variety of wildlife – bear, moose, elk, deer, and buffalo – in this section of the Alcan.

The scenery may not be as spectacular as the descent from Stone Mountain, but there are more mountains just ahead. After skirting the stone pillars and winding through the high draws, Muncho Lake is right in front of you – truly one of the most beautiful bodies of water, anywhere. Follow along the water's edge and stop pretty much as you please as there are many turn-outs.

On the north end of the Lake is Double G Services, which was closed when we past here last. Also, on the north end you will find **Strawberry Flats Campground**, which does not have RV services. Further on is **Northern Rockies Lodge,** where the facilities as advertised include a hotel, fully licensed dining room and lounge, motel, cozy cabins, lakeshore chalets, RV campground, sauna and a gas station. There are some publications which advertise **Muncho Lake RV Park**. However, we believe this RV park is now closed.

After leaving the Lake, just a short distance further (38 miles) is **Laird River Hot Springs and Laird River Provincial Park.** The campground is open year-round and the amenities include: bathing pools, change houses, wheelchair access, a playground, and a 300-meter long, wooden walkway leading from the parking lot to the hot springs pool, crossing picturesque muskeg. **Laird Hotsprings Lodge** has an excellent reputation as a stopping place with rooms and RV park. If you do stop here, ask about Trapper Ray and the "fur-bearing spiders."

Another hour of driving, assuming you do not

stop for buffalo on the road, brings you to **Coal River Park**. This facility, open from May to September, provides 21 full-service sites, showers and washrooms, a laundromat, a motel, and a restaurant. Fuel is generally available.

Buffalo use the Alcan to trail between foraging areas. Their size and weight gains them the right-of-way.

Moving on you will come to Fireside. There may be signs indicating services are available here, but we have observed this location to be closed for several years. The next stop of interest is near Contact Creek. You have been enjoying the drive traveling on a very good road looking for animals and aware that you are reaching ever closer to your destination – north. You round a slight turn and the sign on the right side of the road says: "**Welcome to Yukon**." It's been a great trip so far, and there's a lot more to come.

Sign greeting you as you enter the Yukon Territory.

The sign also indicates that Iron Creek is just 12 miles ahead. However, this facility is closed. The next place for services is **Contact Creek** which does not have an RV park, but there is parking available if you need to rest or arrive late at night. Some of the services available include a coffee shop, snacks, gas and diesel, car repair, and towing. As you travel on, you will find that your stay in the Yukon is short lived as the Alcan dips back down into British Columbia.

Approximately half-way from the initial border crossing into the Yukon is **Hyland River Provincial Park**. There are no facilities for electricity or water connections. The next place for RV and tourist services is Watson Lake.

Watson Lake to Whitehorse

The **"Sign Post City"** at Watson Lake offers full services for the RV tourist. We suggest you research a little bit about this unique exhibition. You just might want to take your own sign along with you.

The Sign Post Forest, also known as "Sign Post City," is an interesting spot to stop and stretch your legs.

We are aware of only one RV park: **Downtown RV Park Watson Lake**. It provides full services but does not provide tenting. On the north side of Watson Lake is Upper Laird which is closed.

Seven miles beyond is Junction 37 Services, where you will find the **Baby Nugget RV Park**. It has 90 pull-through RV hook-up sites – electricity and water. The majority of these sites are 30-amp, but they do have a few 50-amp sites as well. In addition, the Baby Nugget RV Park has a laundromat, RV wash, Wi-Fi access, a gift shop, and a non-denominational church. Furthermore, if your RV has any problems, there is an on-site RV mechanic.

At Mile 710 is the **Rancheria Lodge – RV Park** which offers very large campsites with electricity hook-ups. However due to damage from prior flooding, repairs to the water service are still in progress (as of 2013). The lodge works up some great meals or a cool afternoon drink. We believe fuel may be available.

The next location for RV services is **Walker's Continental Divide Lodge.** There is an RV park with 32 sites including pull-through spots and a sani-dump. Other amenities include showers, laundromat, café, and gift shop. Fuel is available.

Another two hours, plus or minus, will bring you to Teslin. On the way there are three places which may be advertised, but as of 2013 they were all closed. They are Swift River, Morley River, and Dawson Peaks. We are unable to confirm if these facilities will be open in the future.

Teslin is a good stopping point with adequate services for the RV tourist. This Good Sam RV park is part of the **Yukon Motel** and is located on the shore of Nisutlin Bay in a mosquito-controlled area, just a stone's throw away from the restaurant, souvenir shop, and wildlife museum. Amenities available include: 70 sites, full and partial hook-ups, 40 pull through sites, a dump station (free with fuel fill-up), and cleaning facilities – shower house and laundromat. Fuel is always available.

You may see many signs advertising "Mukluk Annie's" for salmon bake and RV services. Unfortunately, this well-known stopping place has been closed for several years. There is a place named Timberpoint Campground, but it does not provide overnight camping – only long-term leased sites.

Another victim of the times, **Johnson's Crossing** on the Alaska Highway has closed their business as of the spring of 2013. Just past Johnson's crossing is **Segunda Lake** where there may be camping. We have no information on this site.

The next location on your excursion north is **Jake's Corner** which offers a restaurant and bakery.

Fuel should be available.

Midway from Jake's Corner to Whitehorse is **Marsh Lake Campground**. There are no RV services here.

There are plenty of good places to pull off and partake of the scenic grandeur of the Rocky Mountains.

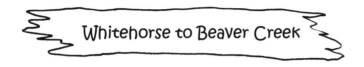

Whitehorse to Beaver Creek

As you approach Whitehorse, the **Caribou RV Park,** a Good Sam park with full RV services, will be on your right. In addition to this park, Whitehorse offers three other RV parks:

Pioneer RV Park
Mountain Ridge Motel and RV Park
HI Country RV Park

Whitehorse, the capital of the Yukon, has every service one could imagine. It is a great town to venture around and get the feel of "gold fever."

Before you leave this city you might make a decision: the Alcan direct to Alaska OR the Klondike Highway to Dawson City. If you decide on the latter, you can continue on to Alaska via the Top of the World Highway. We advise inquiring with the local tourist office in Whitehorse as to the condition of this highway. For the most part, this highway is not paved in Alaska and is subject to deterioration in the event of heavy rains. There is a no cost ferry to take you across the Yukon River. Be aware that the

Alaska Customs Station is not open 24 hours per day. Therefore, schedule your travel time so you are not delayed waiting to pass through Customs.

Approximately an hour and one half west of Whitehorse is **Otter Falls Cut Off**. This stop, which is open year-round, offers an RV park, motel, fuel, a convenience store, a laundromat, and showers. Before you reach Haines Junction, there is a campground: **Pine Lake Campground**. It has no RV services.

Haines Junction is a full-service community with two RV parks. **Fas Gas RV Park** is located on the right side of the road as you enter town, and **Kluane RV Campground** (pronounced: clew-wan-nee), a Good Sam Park, is located on the left side of the road just after you make the right turn at the main intersection. You might take note of the signs directing you to the bakery – the treats are great!

You have been impressed with the scenery over the past few days: Stone Mountain, Summit Lake, Muncho Lake and all the vistas along the way. Be prepared for even more dazzling displays of nature's beauty.

As you depart Haines Junction, you may experience a discomfort with your tow vehicle. It may seem that there's something wrong. Hopefully, it's a result of the gradual climb through the foothills. We get fooled every year. The next part of your adventure (at least one hour to Cottonwood RV Park) will bring you to the shores of Kluane Lake – have your cameras ready and look for the pull-offs. There is a rest stop at the base of Sheep Mountain. We advise extra caution with your pets. Do not let them run loose – this is serious grizzly country. Over the years, we have seen more grizzlies on this stretch of the highway than any other place. The road has recently been upgraded and no longer follows close to the shore. However, there are several places to take a rest and soak in the majesty.

Cottonwood RV Park, on the shores of beautiful Kluane Lake provides lakeside sites, hook-ups, pull-throughs, tent sites, sani-dump, unmetered hot showers, cabin rental, and Wi-Fi.

Just a bit further is **Congdon Creek Campground.** No tenting is permitted because of bear activity. The sites are very large and on gravel, and the roads are gravel. There are bear-proof garbage bins. There is a central grassy field with one swing set and a picnic shelter. Some sites are arranged near this area. Tables are big. There are no RV facilities.

Further north is **Destruction Bay RV Lodge,** a full RV service, Good Sam facility.

At this point a special note of caution is required. From Destruction Bay to Kluane Wilderness Village (closed) the road is in very good shape. However, depending upon the severity of the winter just past, there may be excessive "frost heaves," more noticeable the further north you travel. The Yukon highway maintenance personnel do a very good job in identifying these frost heaves by placing red flags just off the pavement in the shoulder of the road. When you see one of these flags, and there may be many more to come, slow down – you don't want to hit these rises in the pavement too fast which could result in extensive damage. Until you get to the Alaskan border just west of Beaver Creek, these frost heaves will be ever-present. Many folks forget about the pleasures of driving the Alcan and only remember the frost heaves. Hopefully, your good memories will far outnumber the less than good.

The road meanders and takes you away from the lake but the scenery continues to enthral. Pine Valley Lodge has been closed for several years. **Lake Creek Campground** is another of the many government operated facilities. There are no RV Services. Koidern Creek is probably closed, and Bear Flats is well on the way to archaeology studies. You may want to stop at Bear Flats for an inspection in case you want to invest in this "fixer upper."

You are now heading to the final section of the Alcan in Canada. There are only two more RV parks in the Yukon: **Discovery Yukon Lodgings & RV Park**, also known as **White River RV Park**. It is a Good Sam Park located at Mile 1129. It provides full RV hook-ups. While we have not stayed at this location for several years, we are aware that there have been considerable improvements to the facilities over the past few years.

The next stop, the last in the Yukon, is Beaver Creek. This community may not provide full services in comparison with Whitehorse, but the folks here are very friendly and more than willing to assist in any way they can. As a caution, be sure you don't exceed the speed limits.

There is one RV park, **Westmark Beaver Creek RV Park**, located on the right side of the road as you enter the town. We have stayed here several times and found the facilities to be more than adequate. The hook-ups include electricity and water, and there is a black water dump station.

There is a consideration to be given before you depart Beaver Creek for Alaska. Just across the border in Alaska is an RV park located at Border City. This is not a city. It's a roadside stop with a restaurant, where one can obtain fuel and limited mechanical services. They also have cabins. The actual site of the RV park is situated a considerable distance from the shower and bath facilities. Also, the site is in a low-lying area. Thus, if heavy rains have been or will be in the weather picture, the area may be muddy. Accordingly, you may want to spend the night at Beaver Creek. In Alaska, after Border City, the next RV park is in Tok, which is another 100 miles.

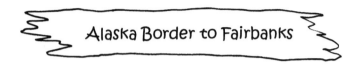

Alaska Border to Fairbanks

Leaving Beaver Creek you will come to the Canadian Customs Station. You are not required to stop but be sure to comply with the speed limits. From the Canadian Customs to the Alaska Border is approximately 20 miles. If you are like us, it seems those last miles just take forever – and the frost heaves do nothing to reduce the anxiety. Just before the hill leading up to the Alaska Customs Station, there is a pull-off area where one can stop to take pictures at the sign shouting to you, "Welcome to Alaska!" You might turn around, look back toward the Yukon, and take a similar picture of another sign, which reads, "Welcome to the Yukon!"

Well, you made it! Welcome to the 49th State, the Last Frontier. The road should be significantly better without the frost heaves you have been bouncing over. Of course, this is subject to how mean the past winter was.

From Border City, and another fuel stop, Scotty Creek, there are no facilities until you reach Tok (pronunciation: rhymes with poke or coke). On the way you will cross several large rivers of which the Tanana (pronounced: Tan-a-naw, not banana) is the largest. It is the drainage for most of the eastern interior of Alaska. Just on the outskirts of Tok, which is a full-service community, you will have cell phone service again. If you are ready for a good lunch or a fine dinner, you might try Fast Eddy's. We always stop and partake of the beer-battered Halibut.

There are three RV parks in Tok:
- **Sourdough Campground**
- **Tok RV Village**
- **Tundra Lodge**

As you leave the Tok area, you will lose cell phone coverage until you reach Delta Junction, also known as Big Delta, which is approximately 100 miles from Tok. The availability of cell phone coverage will be the same at Delta Junction – limited to the city area. Sometime ago this city became the official ending of the Alcan. There is a tourist information center, and you might want to have pictures taken at the milepost.

Delta Junction is another full-service community

and is located approximately 100 miles from Fairbanks. We are aware of only one RV park in Delta Junction: **Smith's Green Acres RV Park,** a Good Sam Park.

Approximately 65 miles from Delta Junction as you travel on to Fairbanks, is the **Knotty Shop**. The reason we mention this particular attraction is the now famous creatures in front of the gift shop. There is ample parking for RV rigs, and you are welcome to have pictures taken – a real treat for young and old alike. You might want to make note of the mileage so you are prepared to make the stop.

The next point of interest is Eielson Air Force Base and then North Pole, the home of **Santa Claus House.** You might have seen advertisements for an RV park here, but the RV park was closed after 2010. There is an RV park just to the west towards Fairbanks. It is named **Riverview RV Park**, a Good Sam Park. It's located about ten minutes from downtown Fairbanks. This is a good location to drop your rig and tour the area. It is located just a few minutes west of North Pole on Badger Road, West (follow the signs, exiting to the right).

If you are looking for the best restaurant in the

area, don't pass up the **Pagoda Chinese Restaurant** in North Pole, located in the Safeway parking lot, next to Key Bank at the intersection of the Alcan (Richardson Highway) and Badger Road (East).

One additional tip: If you are a member of The Elks Lodge, BPOE, you might wish to inquire about the use of their RV parking facilities located at the Elks Lodge in downtown Fairbanks, on the north side of the Chena River. Their number is (907) 456-1551, and they are located at 1003 Pioneer Road].

Updates for 2017 Travel Season

The 2017 travel season may be the right time for your trip to Alaska. The cost of fuel as of the first of the year was slightly higher than the same time last year and all indications suggest continuing low fuel prices through the foreseeable future.

This past year (2016) we departed for the Great Land on May 15 and returned on August 25. We encountered no difficulties from Missouri to Canada and on to Dawson Creek, the start of the Alaska Highway. From Dawson Creek to Fairbanks we had good weather, good roads and a safe travel. We are pleased to report the road conditions as of August 2016 are very good all the way to Alaska. However, there is always one exception: The last 200 km (120 miles) before the Alaskan border have varying degrees of rough surface and pavement breaks. The frost heaves may be rather severe for about 186 km (116 miles) starting just north of Destruction Bay.

We again took the bypass around Calgary and this is great! As you approach Calgary look for direction signs for the Deerfoot Trail and follow the signage to Highway 201 East. Do not get on the Deerfoot Trail. Instead, look for the sign: **Stony Trail – 201 North**. This is an excellent new highway. However, so far there are no fuel stations until you are past the Calgary area. The first fuel stations will be just off the right side of the highway not too far past Calgary.

We also took the bypass around Grand Prairie, primarily to avoid the numerous red/green lights and the traffic. As you approach the Grand Prairie outer perimeter, the first intersection will give choices to Peace River or Grand Prairie. To bypass the city of Grand Prairie, continue straight through the first intersection. Initially, there are no highway marker signs, but the divided highway continues straight.

After ½ mile, a green sign identifies Dawson Creek as a destination. Continue straight and follow the signs identifying a left turn on Highway 43X. Turn left onto 43X and continue straight until you reach an intersection with Highway 43. Note: there are two small, green signs indicating the correct way (right turn) to get to the Alaska Highway.

The highway from the Canadian border north to Dawson Creek is excellent without construction areas (as of August 2016.) The first section of expected construction will be on the hill leading down to the Peace River and the city of Taylor. Construction was still under way in August 2016. However, we encountered no delays, and we anticipate the same on our northward travel in May 2017.

There is a pull off for truckers to check their brakes. If you require a rest or need to check your vehicle, do so before starting the decline.

We encountered road construction on this hill on our travel north in May. On our return trip in August (2016), the construction work had expanded considerably. Traveling south towards Dawson Creek is less daunting as the direction is uphill. However, for those traveling north we advise **extreme caution**. Construction workers and equipment may cause delays and certainly will require a significant slowdown in speed and possibly complete stoppage until workers and equipment are out of the roadway. Such stoppage for equipment will probably be for short durations. Be prepared to follow all directions and cautions. You don't want to be going too fast and be unable to stop. Use caution and be safe.

It may well be that the construction is completed by spring 2017. However, we doubt this will be the case. It appears that the construction will continue well into 2017. The construction at the descent to the Peace River is the only major construction work we encountered on the Alcan Highway.

We took some time to explore some of the RV Parks between the US/Canada border and Edmonton. There are a lot of parks to choose from with many municipalities and/or groups such as the Lions Club operating from May through September. Be aware that a few of these places do not have water hookups at each site. We suspect this is due to the cost of maintenance during the very cold winters. They do provide a central filling location where arrivals can add fresh drinking water.

Another thing to know is that many of the RV parks require the use of coins to activate the showers. In Canada, the most common coin required is a "loonie." This is a Canadian dollar, so called because of the relief of a loon on the obverse side. The Canadians also have a two-dollar coin which is called a "two-nny," even though there are no loons on this coin. Generally, these coins may be purchased at the check-in desk of the RV parks.

We found a VISA card through our bank which does not charge a foreign transaction fee for purchases made outside of the US. We used this card on our trip in 2016 without encountering problems at the pump. In the past, the pump(s) would not read our card(s). This new card has a chip embedded, and we had no problems at the pumps which read credit cards. Check with your bank.

We will be departing again for Alaska in mid-May of 2017. Anyone traveling after this date may contact us via email at RV2AK@yahoo.com for the latest road conditions and updates.

We spent the summer of 2016 staying at an RV Park in Fairbanks. In past years we have parked our Travel Trailer in the front yard of our son's home right in town. We conceded to his request for a season whereby his yard would produce grass. So, our stay from May through mid-August found us located at Riverview RV Park Campground.

We are pleased to be able to give it a Five Star PLUS recommendation to one and all who travel via RV/Camping to the Fairbanks/North Pole area. This is a Good Sam Park managed by a professional team which really cares, and they give special attention to all the little details that will make your stay a pleasant experience. Maximum effort is made to provide some form of no-cost entertainment three times each week. This past year we entertained one and all three evenings each week, and we plan on doing the same in 2017. Come join in the fun, we would be pleased to meet you and "cuss and discuss" anything and everything about your trip to Alaska.

The facilities are exceptionally clean with bath and shower and laundry facilities cleaned daily. The whole area has more than plentiful grass and a superb area for walking the four-legged friends. The "pull-thrus" are easily accessible with the utility stands and sewer drains in the most convenient locations.

We highly recommend you contact Riverview RV Park Campground early and make reservations. Spaces may be in short supply from early June through mid-August. Take a view of their web page at www.riverviewrvpark.net.

Reservations. As mentioned above, this past year we stayed at an RV Park instead of in town. One of the things we learned and wish to pass on to you is the matter of reservations. We make every effort to speak with fellow traveling RVers and learn something new. We learned that RV Parks in Alaska become very crowded during the heart of the summer (mid-June through July.) As such, we highly recommend you inquire with each RV Park in which you wish to stay as to availability for the days you will be staying there. This is especially true at those locations with high attendance such as Fairbanks, Denali and Mt. McKinley as well as locations on the Kenai Peninsula, Homer and Valdez.

If you have the time, please stop and let's visit for a while. If there is anything we can do to make your trip more memorable, we will make every effort to comply with your needs.

      Be safe, Rich and Gloria
      Email address: RV2AK@yahoo.com

Appendix I

Publications and Websites

Bell's Travel Guide. This is an excellent guide with a very good section maps and is available at almost every location starting with Dawson Creek. You can get it ahead of time at the following address:
>*Bell's Travel Guides* (Free)
>1770 Front St. #170
>Lynden, WA 98264
>Administration: (250) 768-2426

The Mile Post Magazine. *The Mile Post Magazine* is an excellent travel guide. However, we feel there is chance to "over-due" the travel experience. But that should not stop or deter anyone from getting maximum information. We have never utilized this travel guide, but we know of many who would not travel the Alcan without it. You find it online at:
>http://www.tips-for-backwoods-alaska-vacations.com/milepost-magazine.html

Yukon Trip Planner. This is a tour planning and

reservation website. It lists upcoming events. You can find it at http://www.yukon.worldweb.com/

Yukon – Larger than Life. This is another good Yukon travel planning website. It lists accommodations, events, sights to see, and other travel info. It is online at http://travelyukon.com/

Wikipedia: List of Canada – United States border crossings. This article contains a list of border crossings. It gives hours of service and other pertinent information. You can find the entry at:
    http://en.wikipedia.org/wiki/List_of_Canada-United_States_border-crossings.

For further information on RV travel, RV parks, campgrounds, or the Alcan in general, take some time and search the web – there's quite a bit of information waiting for you to click on.

If we can be of further assistance in any way or if you have specific questions or want to know the most current road conditions, e-mail us, Rich and Gloria Eskew, at RV2AK@yahoo.com .

Appendix II

List of RV Parks

Whitecourt:
- Lion's Club RV Park – Good Sam
- Sagitawah RV Park – Good Sam
- Fox Creek RV Campground

Valleyview:
- Sands Wilderness
- Sherk's RV Park - Good Sam

Grand Prairie:
- Country Roads RV Park - Good Sam
- Legion Park
- Camp Tamarack RV Park Inc. - Good Sam
- Stampede Campground & R.V. Park
- Nitehawk Rotary RV Park - Good Sam
- Grande Prairie Rotary RV Park
- Beaverlodge Pioneer Campground,
- Hythe Municipal Campground.

Dawson Creek:
- Alahart RV & Tent Park
- Farmington Fairways RV Resort
- Mile 0 Campground - Good Sam
- Northern Lights RV Park - Good Sam
- Tubby's RV Park

Taylor, Fort St. John, Charlie Lake:
- Peace Island Regional Park Campground
- Fairway RV Park
- Ross H. Maclean Rotary RV Park

Shepherd's Inn
Sasquatch Crossing - Sportsman's Inn
Sikanni Chief Campground and RV Park - Good Sam

Fort Nelson:
Triple "G" Hideaway RV Park & Rest. - Good Sam
Blue Bell Inn RV
Toad River Lodge - Good Sam
Northern Rockies Lodge
Laird Hotsprings Lodge
Coal River Park
Hyland River Provincial Park
Downtown RV Park Watson Lake - Good Sam
Junction 37 Services
Baby Nugget RV Park - Good Sam
Rancheria Lodge - RV Park
Walker's Continental Divide Lodge
Yukon Motel (Teslin) - Good Sam

Whitehorse:
Caribou RV Park - Good Sam
Pioneer RV Park - Good Sam
Mountain Ridge Motel and RV Park
HI Country RV Park - Good Sam
Otter Falls Cut Off

Haines Junction:
Fas Gas (Haines Junction) & RV Park
Kluane R.V. Kampground
Cottonwood RV Park
Destruction Bay RV Lodge - Good Sam
Discovery Yukon Lodgings & RV Park (White River RV Park) - Good Sam

Beaver Creek:
Westmark Beaver Creek RV
Sourdough Campground

Border City RV Park (Alaska)
Tok, Alaska:
Tok RV Village - Good Sam
Tundra Lodge
Delta Junction, Alaska:
Smith's Green Acres RV Park - Good Sam
North Pole, Alaska:
Riverview RV Park Campground - Good Sam

Index

Alaska Border to Fairbanks: 100-103
Alcan Highway: 1-109
Ammunition: 22
Bearings – trailer: 35-40, 51
Black water drain: 46, 99
Border crossings: 19-23, 105
Brakes – controller: 43-44
Bumper add-ons: 46-47
Calgary bypass: 31
Canada Day: 23
Canadian coins 108
Canadian Customs: 19-23
Canadian Customs at Couts: 19
Canadian Customs at Del Bonita: 20
Cell Phones: 14, 25-26, 28, 101
Checklist: 60-61
Citizen's Band (CB) radio: 26-27
Communications Canada: 25-29
Credit Cards: 14, 24-25, 108
Currency in Canada: 24-25
Cut Bank to Del Bonita: 17-18, 20
Dawson City: 94
Dawson Creek to Fort Nelson: 75-81
Dawson Creek, British Columbia: 75-76
Deerfoot Trail, Calgary: 31
Devon, Alberta: 18, 32
Diary: 55
DUI: 21-22
Edmonton bypass: 18, 32
Edmonton to Dawson Creek: 70-74
Electricity hook-up: 43, 50, 52-53
Engines: 35
Explain TV operations: 54, 60
Extra level blocks: 54-55
Fire extinguishers: 51
Firearms – weapons: 22-23
Fort Nelson to Watson Lake: 82-89
Fresh water: 48-49
Fuel cards: 107-108
Fuses: 53-54
Getting-there route through U.S.: 14-19
Good Sam Club-road hazard service: 12-13
GPS: 28-29
Hitch: 44-45
Hot water heater" 49
Hours of operations at border crossings: 105
Insurance: 12-13, 20-21
Klondike Highway: 94
Leduc, Alberta: 18, 31-32
Level braces: 47
List of essentials: 50-51

Mace: 23
Medications: 12
Mileage and facilities: 63-66
Passports: 14, 20-21
Pepper spray: 23
Pets: 21, 60, 96
Photocopies: 13-14
Power hitch: 44-45
Prescriptions (medicine and vision): 12, 14
Pressure monitors: 42-43
Propane: 45-46, 61
Reservations: 11, 105
Road hazard service insurance: 12-13
RV Manuals: 12
Safety: 43, 51-52
Sirius: 28-29
Small animal certificate: 14, 21
Showers – coins: 108
Storage – organize: 49-51

Tips and suggestions: 55-63, 104
Tire pressure monitors: 42-43
Tires: 33, 40-42, 57
Travel in Alberta: 19
Travel – best months: 67
Travel around Calgary: 31
Travel around Edmonton: 18, 32
Traveling in Canada: 23-33
Traveling in Northwest Alberta: 32-33
Vehicle registrations: 14, 20
Water pipes – access: 49
Watson Lake to Whitehorse: 90-93
Weather: 7, 27, 34, 78, 99
What to take: 49-51
Whitehorse to Beaver Creek: 94-99
Wi-Fi access: 27-28, 91, 96
Window seals: 47-48

About the Authors

Rich and Gloria found each other while living in Alaska – a Director of Nursing meets a business executive – and their life together has been one great adventure. Collectively, they have traveled the Alcan seventy-three times in pickups, sedans, cargo trailers, and travel trailers. In their book, *RVing North to Alaska*, they expertly pass on many of the details of RV and Alcan travel so commonly overlooked.

Currently, they reside most of the year in Springfield, Missouri, with two annual trips to Virginia to visit their daughter and the grandkids. Every May they can be seen on the road heading north to Alberta, British Columbia, The Yukon, and on to Fairbanks to spend the summer with their son and grandkids. All along the way, especially on the Alcan, friendships are renewed while new acquaintances become forever friends.

Rich Eskew is a novelist and poet. Among his publications which are sold on three continents are:
> *A Tale of Three Journeys*
> *Memories from the Muck*
> *Walk With Me*
> *Legends, Tall Tales and Outright Lies*

In his developed persona as "Griz Bait," Rich performs on stage delighting audiences with tales of hilarity, historical accounts of the Gold Rush era, and true-life adventures.

Made in the USA
Lexington, KY
03 March 2017